HOANG ANH
A VIETNAMESE-AMERICAN BOY

 Published by Scholastic Inc., 730 Broadway, New York, NY 10003, by arrangement with Holiday House, Inc.
Printed in the U.S.A.
ISBN 0-590-47394-8
ISBN 0-590-29131-9 (meets NASTA specifications)

9 10 08 6 7 8 9/0

ACKNOWLEDGMENTS

In creating this book, we enjoyed the cooperation and enthusiasm of many people. We would like to express our appreciation to the entire Chau family—Thao, Phuong Lam, Tung, Binh, Tu Anh, Tuan, and especially Hoang Anh—for their participation in this project and for sharing their story with us; to Midzung Bui, for her help in translating; and to Phuc Huu Tran, who brought the cultural beauty of Vietnam to life for us.

We would also like to thank Barbara Belluomini and the students in her classroom at the Davidson Middle School in San Rafael for their participation; and Duong Bui of Monterey, and Chieu Pham of the Vietnamese Fisherman Association of America, for their help in the early stages of our research.

HOANG ANH
A VIETNAMESE-AMERICAN BOY

BY DIANE HOYT-GOLDSMITH

PHOTOGRAPHS BY LAWRENCE MIGDALE

SCHOLASTIC INC.
New York Toronto London Auckland Sydney

This book is dedicated to our children,
Aaron and Leah Goldsmith,
and Daniel Migdale.

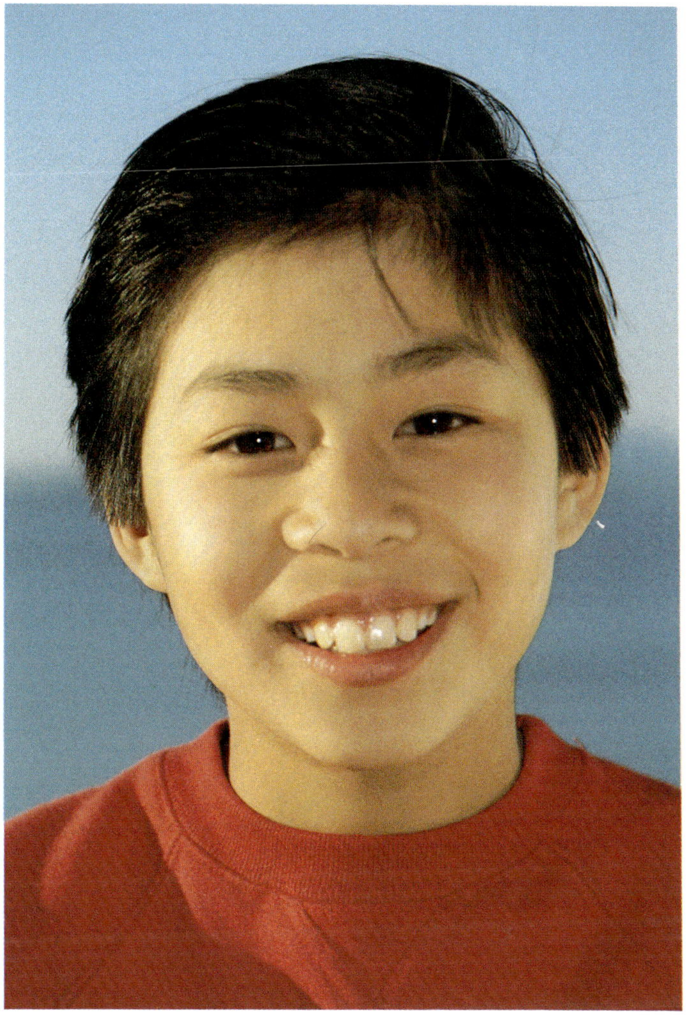

My name is Hoang Anh Chau *(WONG ON CHOH)*. I live in the town of San Rafael, California. In our home, we speak two languages: Vietnamese and English. I came to this country with my family when I was just a baby. We are all refugees from Vietnam, here to begin a new life. My parents, my older brothers, my sister, and I are new citizens of the United States. We are Vietnamese-Americans.

How We Came

Hoang Anh's father raises the wire crab trap with a winch and cable that is powered by electricity. The white plastic cup in the center holds the bait.

My father, Thao Chau *(TAU CHOH)*, is a fisherman. On days when the weather is good, he gets up at three o'clock in the morning. He goes to his boat and heads out to the ocean. Working hard all day, my father visits the places where he has set traps to catch crabs and eels. Usually, he doesn't get home until long after dark. My father learned to be a fisherman in Vietnam.

My parents came from a small town called Kieng Giang *(KEENG JANG)* on the Mekong *(MAY-KONG)* Delta in the southern part of Vietnam. In that region, there are many rice farms. My father, like his father before him, owned a tractor and earned a living by plowing the fields for farmers.

But in 1977, my parents made a decision that changed their lives. They decided to leave Vietnam.

My father had been a soldier in the South Vietnamese army since 1971. For years, he had fought alongside the Americans against the Communist forces led by North Vietnam. During the war, many of my father's friends and relatives were killed. He watched as the war destroyed homes, farms, and towns. He saw that his way of life was changing forever.

Unable to defeat the Communists, the United States sent its soldiers home in 1973. Two years later, the Communists of North Vietnam took control of the entire country. The new government acted harshly toward people like my father who had fought against them. My parents were frightened for their own safety. They worried about the future. They wanted to raise their children in a better place.

The Communist government of Vietnam, however, would not allow people to leave the country. So my parents planned secretly to escape from Vietnam and seek a new life of safety and freedom in the United States. In doing so, they would become refugees.

To carry out his plan, my father sold his tractor and bought a small fishing boat. He learned to fish, working in the waters of the Gulf of Thailand. He had a plan to escape, but he did not want the Vietnamese government to become suspicious. He watched and waited for the right time.

Then one day in 1978, my parents gathered together some food and clothing for a long journey. They said goodbye to their parents and their friends. In the dark of the night, my parents brought their four young children on board the small fishing boat. With his family and twenty-four other refugees hidden below the deck, my father sailed away from the shores of Vietnam.

Happy that the morning's catch was good, Hoang Anh helps his father put the crabs into a tall barrel. His father will take the crabs to a fish market in San Francisco, where they will be sold.

A news clipping shows the Chau family shortly after their arrival in the United States. Hoang Anh, on his mother's lap, is still a small baby. His father and a brother sit on the couch and his aunt stands in the doorway behind.

He pretended it was just another day of fishing. But when the little boat reached the open water, he did not stop to put out the crab traps. Sailing west and south, he kept on going toward the island nation of Malaysia.

My brothers and sister were much too young to realize what was happening. They had no idea of the danger they were in. The small, overcrowded boat faced many hardships on the journey. It could have been lost at sea. It could have been swamped in a terrible storm. The passengers could have run out of food and water before reaching land again. Worst of all, sea pirates could have discovered the boat and taken everybody's belongings and even their lives.

But my family was lucky. After two days and two nights on the ocean, they reached Malaysia safely. For more than a year, they lived in a camp for refugees. It was filled with many other people who had fled from Vietnam. Conditions in the camp were very poor. There was little food to eat and nothing for people to do.

It was in this refugee camp in Malaysia that I was born. In spite of the poor conditions there, I was a very healthy baby. When I was a few months old, a church in Oregon sponsored my family, and we emigrated to the United States.

I have read in books that over a million people fled from Vietnam after the war because they were frightened about what the country would be like under a Communist government. Many of these "boat people" made it to safety, as my family did. But many more were shipwrecked and had to be rescued by passing boats. Some were discovered by the Communist government and sent back to Vietnam. The most unfortunate people were those who met pirate ships. They were robbed, beaten, kidnapped, sold as slaves, or even tossed overboard. As a result many refugees have just disappeared completely.

Sometimes, when I help my father at the docks, I look at his fishing boat and think about his daring escape. The boat that carried my family away from Vietnam was ten feet shorter in length, yet it brought thirty people to a new life. My parents were very brave to have taken such risks to bring us all to the United States.

Hoang Anh's father fishes from this boat. It is much larger than the boat that brought his family and many other refugees out of Vietnam.

Hoang Anh and his family eat some of the same foods in the United States as they did in Vietnam. They often enjoy fish and seafood as a main course for the evening meal.

LIFE AT HOME

Often, my father brings home some fresh crab or Cua *(KOO-AH)* for us to eat. An ordinary evening meal at our home in California is like an ordinary evening meal anywhere in Vietnam. We eat many of the same foods here.

At our table, we use deep rice bowls instead of plates, and chopsticks instead of forks, knives, and spoons. First, we might have a soup called Canh bi Dao *(CAN BEE DOW)* made from sliced squash, pork, and onions. With that, we have Suon Ram *(SOON RAM)*, which is pork ribs prepared with fish sauce. Usually, we eat some type of fish or seafood as a main course, and there is always lots of rice or Com *(KOLM)*.

My favorite American food is pizza, but I like to make a Vietnamese snack for myself after school. I cut up a fresh cucumber and dip the slices in nuoc mam *(NOOK MAM)*, a spicy, brown fish sauce. Vietnamese people use this sauce with lots of different foods, the same way Americans use catsup.

In Vietnam, only women work in the kitchen. But here, my family has adopted an American life-style. Everyone in our household knows how to cook.

My mother, Phuong Lam *(FONG LAM)*, has a full-time job outside our home. She works six and occasionally seven days a week at a beauty shop doing manicures for people. Because she doesn't get home until quite late in the evening, we all help out. Sometimes my father makes dinner. He has learned to be a good cook.

There are five children in our family, and I am the youngest. My older brothers are named Tung *(TUNG)*, Binh *(BIN), and* Tuan *(TWAN)*. My sister's name is Tu Anh *(TOO ON)*.

All of us are busy with school. I go to junior high school, Tu Anh and Tuan are in high school, and Tung and Binh attend college. My brothers and sister each have a part-time job as well.

As in all of Southeast Asia, rice is a staple food for the Vietnamese people.

In Hoang Anh's classroom, the students are making maps of the countries in Southeast Asia.

In my school, there are many children who come from other parts of the world and speak English as a second language. There are kids from Mexico, Central America, China, and the Middle East. Two of my best friends are from Kampuchea (Cambodia), a country in Southeast Asia near Vietnam.

Our life in the United States is good, but like most families, we have problems too. My parents, my brothers, and my sister work hard to earn enough money to buy the things we need and want. But when the crab season is over, my father is out of a job for several months. That puts more pressure on the rest of us.

Although my father understands English well, he still has trouble speaking it. This makes it hard for him to find another job. I know how frustrated he feels because it is hard for me to switch from speaking Vietnamese at home to speaking English at school.

The Vietnamese language is quite different from English. In the Vietnamese alphabet, there is no f, j, w or z. Most of our letters are pronounced differently from how they sound in English. And some English sounds do not exist at all in Vietnamese.

Ours is a tonal language. This means that the pitch of the word is important to its meaning. In Vietnamese, most words have but one syllable. Each word has a distinct pitch, high or low, like a note on a musical scale. For example, the word *ma* can have six different meanings depending upon the pitch. It can mean *rice seedling, that* or *but, tomb* or *grave, ghost, horse,* or *mommy.*

I'm still too young to get a regular job, so I help out around the house as much as I can. Sometimes I get my father's fishing gear ready. I try to keep my room neat. And I help to water the trees and shrubs in the yard.

For several years, California has suffered from a drought. Not enough rain has fallen and the reservoirs are low. Water has become very scarce. This was never a problem for my parents in Vietnam, where it always rains a lot.

Sometimes Hoang Anh helps his father with his fishing gear. These floats will mark the places where the crab traps are put in the ocean.

Hoang Anh's cousin helps him water the plants in the yard. The solar panels on the roof help to heat water for their home.

My father thought of a good way to save water during the rainy season to use later in the year. He made a storage area along the north side of our house. Stacking up empty plastic buckets to catch the rain, he made his own small reservoir. By carefully watering our shrubs with what we collect from the rains, I help to keep our water bills low.

Most of the time, I'm like any American kid. I like to ride my bike and listen to rap music with my friends. I go roller skating and play video games with my cousins on weekends. I dream about becoming a professional football player when I grow up, so I throw the football every chance I get. I would also like to be an artist.

One of Hoang Anh's favorite pastimes is playing football with his brothers.

GLOSSARY

Ao dai: *(Ow Zai)* Traditional Vietnamese garment with long sleeves and a high collar. Usually made of silk or brocade, the garment is open at the sides below the waist and is worn over loose trousers. The style for men and women is the same.
Banh chung: *(Bon Choong)* A square cake made from rice, mung beans, and a mixture of meat, and wrapped in banana leaves.
Banh day: *(Bon Zay)* A round, dome-shaped cake made of plain rice.
Calligrapher: A person who practices the art of beautiful handwriting, usually with a brush.
Canh bi Dao: *(Can Bee Dow)* A Vietnamese soup made with sliced squash, onions, and pork.
Chopsticks: Two long narrow sticks, usually made from wood or ivory, that are used as eating utensils throughout Asia. Chopsticks originated in China.
Chuc Mung Nam Moi: *(Chook Mung Nam Moi)* means "Happy New Year" in Vietnamese.
Chu nho: *(Choo Nyaw)* A system of writing also called the Southern Script. It has been used in Vietnam by scholars for many centuries.
Com: *(Kolm)* The Vietnamese term for rice.
Communism: A system of government in which the public controls the production and distribution of all goods and services.
Cua: *(Koo-ah)* The Vietnamese word for crab.
Dynasty: A line of rulers from the same family.
Emigrate: To move from one country or place to another.
Kieng Giang: *(Keeng Jang)* A town in Vietnam on the Mekong Delta.
Loc: *(Low)* A Vietnamese term meaning Wealth.
Longevity: Long life.
Lunar month: The time between one full moon and the next full moon, approximately 29½ days.
Lunar year: Made up of twelve lunar months, or approximately 354 days.
Lunar new year: Begins on the second new moon after the beginning of winter, no earlier than January 20 and no later than February 20.
Malaysia: A nation composed of hundreds of tiny islands in Southeast Asia.
Martial arts: A method of unarmed combat or self-defense.
Marquetry: The art of creating designs or pictures by cutting and gluing thin pieces of colored wood.
Mekong Delta: *(May-kong)* A rich agricultural region in Vietnam at the end of the Mekong River. Rice is a major crop on the delta.
Mung beans: A small yellow bean which is made into a sweet paste and used in the recipe for banh chung.
Nuoc mam: *(Nook Mam)* A spicy, brown fish sauce eaten with many Vietnamese dishes.
Palaquin: *(Pal-ah-keen)* A covered chair, usually for one person, carried on the shoulders of two or more men.
Phuc: *(Fook)* means prosperity in the Vietnamese language.
Prosperity: To enjoy wealth, happiness, and success. In the Vietnamese tradition, a person is prosperous if he has many children.
Quoc To Hung Vuong: *(Kwuck Too Hoong Vuong)* The first person to rule Vietnam after its independence from China.
Refugee: A person who flees from his homeland because of war or danger and seeks safety in another place.
Southeast Asia: An area in Asia consisting of these countries: Vietnam, Kampuchea (Cambodia), Myanmar (Burma), Indonesia, Malaysia, Philippines, Singapore, Thailand, and Laos.
Tae Kwon Do *(Tie Kwon Doe)* A type of martial arts developed in Asia.
TET Nguyen-Dan: *(Tet Win-Dahn)* The Feast of the First Day or the Vietnamese New Year Celebration.
Tho: *(Tah)* The Vietnamese word for Longevity.
Tonal language: A language in which the meaning of the word can depend upon the pitch or tone in which it is spoken.
Trang Nguyen: *(Trong Nwin)* The name given the scholar who has scored the highest on the emperor's examinations.
Vietnam: A country in Southeast Asia.

The New Year

There is a special time each year when we celebrate our Vietnamese heritage. This is the New Year, called TET Nguyen-Dan *(TET NWIN-DAHN)*, which means the Feast of the First Day. TET is our most important holiday. We celebrate it for three days, and it's like having Thanksgiving, Christmas, and New Year's all at once.

During TET, I really feel like I am a part of the Vietnamese community in America. I can experience a little of what my family remembers from their life in Vietnam, see old friends and relatives, and learn more about my heritage. But best of all, I can have a lot of fun.

The celebration of TET, like many of our other traditions, has been influenced greatly by Chinese culture. For nearly ten centuries, the Chinese ruled in Vietnam, so our religion, philosophy, literature, and customs are much like theirs. Vietnam has its own language, but even now the traditional scholars read and write in chu nho *(CHOO NYAW)*, a script that looks like the characters in Chinese.

The people of Vietnam use the Chinese calendar, which is based on the moon. TET falls between January 20 and February 20 each year. It begins on the first day of the first month of the lunar year. TET celebrates the birth of spring and the promise of the future.

My family thinks of TET as a new beginning. It is traditional for us to prepare for the holiday by cleaning our house from top to bottom. If anything needs fixing, we do the repairs before TET begins. We want to start the New Year with everything in good shape.

Children who live far away from home come back to visit their parents and spend time with their family. During the three days of the TET celebration, everyone tries to stay in a good mood. If people are cross or angry, it could mean bad luck for the rest of the year.

We celebrate TET by wearing our best clothes. My mother and sister like to put on their traditional Vietnamese dress, called ao dai *(OW ZAI)*. Usually made from bright colored fabrics, these dresses are open at the sides from the waist down and are worn over loose pajama-like trousers. Dressing like this shows they feel good about themselves and the future.

The first person who comes into our home or visits after the New Year is very important. He or she sets the tone for the coming year. If the person is wealthy and respected, it means good luck for the people who live in the house. If that same person arrives just after midnight, so much the better.

We stay up late on the eve before TET to greet the New Year. We try to do something good at midnight, because we believe that also brings us luck.

TET is a time for giving and forgiving. We pay off our debts. We forget past mistakes and forgive others. During the celebration of TET, relatives and friends often exchange gifts. In Vietnam, students give presents to their teachers and businesses give a New Year's bonus to employees. Older relatives give special red envelopes to the children. Inside there are lucky coins...and sometimes a dollar or two!

For the holiday, we like to buy little cakes made of rice called banh day *(BON ZAY)* and banh chung *(BON CHOONG)*. The recipe comes to us from the very early days of Vietnam's history. When I was young, my mother told me a legend that explains why we eat these cakes at the New Year.

Children often receive bright red envelopes with money inside as a gift during TET.

CAKES FOR THE NEW YEAR

*Many years ago, the people of Vietnam believed the earth was square and covered by a round dome, the sky. Hung Vuong (*HOONG VUONG*) the Sixth was emperor of the land. He had many wives, as was the custom in those days, and many sons and daughters, too.*

As he grew old and tired, he began to worry about which of his many sons should succeed him. He wanted to choose the one who would rule the land most wisely.

Living at the court, his sons had an easy life. They did not know very much about the lives of the common country folk. Finally, after much thought, the emperor made up a good test.

He gathered his sons together and said, "Go out into the countryside. In all of Vietnam, find me a food I have never tasted before, a dish that is both delicious and unusual. One year from this day, I will choose the next emperor of the land."

*All of his sons scattered to every corner of the country... all except the youngest, Lang Lieu (*LANG LOO*). He was a sensitive boy, a good hunter, and also a poet. He enjoyed challenges, but this time, he did not want to leave home.*

Lang Lieu had a nursemaid who had cared for him since his mother had died at his birth. Now she was old and ill. Lang Lieu worried that if he left her bedside, she would die. So each day, he tended to her kindly and thought about the emperor's test.

One night, Lang Lieu dreamed of an old man with a snow-white beard. In his dream, the old man said, "In all the earth, there is nothing more precious than rice. Therefore, give the emperor rice. Make it like the heavens and the earth, so that he and all the people will appreciate both."

When Lang Lieu woke, he could think of nothing but the old man's words. Now, when he wasn't at his nursemaid's bedside, he was in the kitchen, cooking the newly harvested rice, trying to create a dish "like the heavens and the earth."

Winter passed and spring arrived. The emperor's sons returned from the countryside. Each one carried a new food. Some foods were spicy and some were sweet, with strange new flavors and colorful ingredients. Tasting each son's offering in turn, the emperor tried them all.

Finally, the emperor came to the last and youngest son. Lang Lieu came forward with several small cakes on a tray. They were wrapped in banana leaves, some round and the others square.

Unwrapping the cakes, the emperor saw that the banana leaves had stained the rice inside a brilliant springtime green. He found a sweet layer of mung beans in the center, the royal color of yellow. The emperor took bite after bite of the delicious concoction. The cakes looked wonderful, but they tasted even better.

"Where did you find out how to make these wonderful cakes when you didn't travel anywhere?" the emperor exclaimed.

Then Lang Lieu told his father about the dream and the words of the old man. He said that the square cakes were like the earth and the round cakes were like the sky.

Now, the emperor knew which of his sons was meant to be the next ruler of Vietnam. Besides being intelligent and kind, Lang Lieu had been lucky enough to get advice from heaven in the form of a dream and had wisely followed it. These qualities made him the best man to rule the land.

So Hung Vuong the Sixth named the square cake banh chung *and the round cake* banh day. *And to this day, the Vietnamese people make these cakes on the New Year to give thanks to the earth for its bounty and to the heavens for their blessings.*

福

Phuc
(Prosperity)

祿

Loc
(Wealth)

壽

Tho
(Longevity)

A Special Visit

In my family, I am the only person who has never lived in Vietnam. I want to learn more about my heritage. I want to know about the culture that was created by my ancestors.

My mother has always told me that education and learning are important to the Vietnamese people. In nearly every village, there is a person of great wisdom who has devoted his life to the pursuit of knowledge. He is called a scholar and is respected and honored.

This year, during the TET celebration, my older brother Binh brought me to meet a scholar from Vietnam. His name is Phuc Huu Tran *(Fook Hoo Trahn)*, and like my family, he came to the United States as a refugee.

For over seventy years he has studied history and philosophy, ethics and geography, literature and poetry. In addition, he has become an excellent calligrapher.

In Vietnam, as in China, a calligrapher practices the art of writing with a brush. He writes each character over and over again, striving for meaning and form. The calligrapher's goal is to make the beauty of the characters match the beauty of the thoughts that they express.

When I first met Phuc Huu Tran, I felt shy. He seemed so different. He was old and wise, like someone you might see in a storybook but not in real life. Speaking in a soft voice, he asked about my family.

After we talked, Phuc Huu Tran wrote out a special New Year's greeting for my parents. Taking a brush and some black ink, he created three characters in chu nho *(Choo Nyaw)*, the Southern Script. He made a few easy strokes with the brush. Although he worked quickly, in the flash of an eye, the characters looked beautiful.

Phuc Tran told me the characters stand for Phuc *(FOOK)*, Loc *(LOW)*, and Tho *(TAH)*. Phuc means Prosperity, Loc means Wealth, and Tho means Longevity.

Hoang Anh watches as Phuc Tran makes characters with his brush.

During our visit, Phuc Tran told me many stories about Vietnam. The one that I like best is a story about the two Trung sisters, who led many battles against the Chinese. This is a true story from Vietnam's history.

At a time when Vietnam was ruled by China, Trung Trac (TRUNG TRACK) *and Trung Nhi* (TRUNG NEE) *were the daughters of a high official in the Vietnamese court. Their father died while the girls were quite young, but their mother made sure they were well educated. She insisted that they be trained in the martial arts as well as in other subjects.*

When Trung Trac came of age, she was married to Thi Sach (TEE SACK). *He was a great military leader, who led a revolution against the Chinese for the independence of Vietnam. Sadly, Thi Sach died in the battle. Sounds of weeping filled the countryside as many other women mourned for their husbands and sons, lost to the war also.*

Trung Trac was angry that her husband's enemies had killed him. She wanted to get even and fight for her country. Her sister, Trung Nhi, decided to join her. Riding on the shoulders of two elephants, the two sisters led the remaining troops into battle. Bravely, other women followed their example, leaving their homes to fight against the enemy. Finally, after many bloody battles, they won freedom for their country.

Because of their bravery and leadership, Trung Trac and Trung Nhi earned great honors. They became Vietnam's first female emperors. After many years, however, their enemies returned to Vietnam with new armies. In the new war, the soldiers led by the Trung sisters were outnumbered. Unwilling to surrender, they fought to the end. Then, knowing they would surely be killed, the Trung sisters flung themselves into the Hat Giang (HAT JANG) *River and drowned.*

At the end of our visit, Phuc Tran gave me the calligraphy he had made to share with my family. I put it in a simple frame as a New Year's gift for my mother. I was proud to give her this treasure from a Vietnamese scholar. In our tradition, *Phuc, Loc,* and *Tho* are the best wishes one can have for the celebration of TET and the beginning of a New Year.

Phuong Lam receives the gift of calligraphy from Hoang Anh as part of the TET New Year's celebration.

The Tet Festival

A sedan chair or palaquin.

My favorite part of the New Year is the TET Festival that is held on the fairgrounds in San Jose, California. Vietnamese people from all over the San Francisco Bay Area come together to celebrate. The community in northern California has one of the largest Vietnamese populations outside of Vietnam, with over 160,000 people.

During the three days of the TET Festival, there are many things to see and do. You can be entertained by variety shows and a beauty pageant. You can go to a concert of music played on classical Vietnamese instruments. For excitement, there are volleyball competitions, a table tennis tournament, and fireworks after dark. There are sideshows and rides on the midway, and games of skill where you can win prizes.

Everywhere you look, people are gathering to have fun. Old men sit together at tables on the lawn and play chess. Students of the martial arts, young and old, practice their routines before going in to face the judges. People of all ages line up in front of the food vendors for a taste of special barbecued pork or chicken with rice.

In the background, the flag of the South Vietnamese government, a yellow field with bright red stripes on it, snaps in the breeze. The festival is also a place where refugees from Vietnam gather to remember the country they left behind. Retired soldiers wear their old uniforms, camouflage jackets, and berets. For them, the war is not forgotten.

Every so often, a palaquin *(PAL-ah-keen)* passes by. This chair is covered by a beautifully decorated box and carried by young men in costume. In Vietnam, the palaquin was used to carry a person of importance.

The palaquins at the TET Festival remind people of Vietnamese village life. It makes them remember that in Vietnam there was a democratic system for advancement. Any person, no matter how humble or poor, could hope to reach the emperor's court if he became well educated.

On the San Jose Fairgrounds, complete with new street signs, the opening ceremonies take place under the TET banner.

Two contestants in a Tae Kwon Do *(TIE KWON DOE)* competition practice their routines. Athletes are judged on their speed, strength, and style.

Because each village had a scholar who could teach different subjects, any child who was eager to learn could study to pass a test. Then he would be able to take a more difficult examination in the nearest city or town.

Every three years, a nationwide exam was given. Those who passed this test were ranked, and the one to score the highest was called Trang Nguyen *(TRONG NWIN)*. This graduate would then be made a high official in the emperor's court.

After the graduate was picked, the emperor would send a message to his village. The student's family would prepare a welcome-home feast for the graduate. Wearing a special cap and gown from the emperor, the graduate would return to his village on horseback, his wife behind him in a palaquin, with the emperor's guard following. Everyone in the village would see the procession.

The graduate would first go to the family altar to pray to Buddha and his ancestors for their blessing. Then he would go to his parents and thank them for their love and support. After feasting and celebrating in the village, the graduate would leave his village for a new career at the palace of the emperor. In this way, the emperor of Vietnam found the brightest and best educated citizens to help to govern the people of the nation.

During TET, people gather in front of booths in the exhibit halls, where many things are for sale. There are toys and encyclopedias, crafts, lovely tropical plants, and orchids. Nearby, an artist who works in marquetry sells tiny landscapes of the Vietnamese countryside. These are made from bits of colored wood, cut and glued together to make a picture. Community groups hand out leaflets to tell about their programs. Public agencies advertise jobs or give advice.

There are beautiful temples set up inside the halls, very much like those you would find on a visit to Vietnam. People

In a booth selling tropical plants, Tu Anh and Hoang Anh try to decide which orchid, among the hundreds for sale, is the most beautiful.

Phuc Tran greets Hoang Anh and shows him the altar he made to honor Vietnam's first emperor, Quoc To Hung Vuong.

go to these temples to pray for peace throughout the world, for good health, and for prosperity in their families.

To show respect for our ancestors, we say prayers and burn incense. For us, the worship of our ancestors is a very important and traditional act. We need to remember where we came from and appreciate the support and love that our parents and grandparents have given us.

Because my family left Vietnam as refugees, I have never met my own grandparents. I have seen them only on the videotape my uncle brought back after his last visit to Vietnam. On our VCR, I watched my grandparents, sitting together on a couch in their home, weeping in front of the camera, overcome by sadness. My uncle filmed them trying to greet us, but a separation of over ten years seemed almost too much for them to bear.

On the last day of the TET Festival, while I wandered through the exhibit halls, I met Phuc Tran again. He was burning incense and praying at an altar he had built to honor Quoc To Hung Vuong *(Kwuck Too Hoong Vuong)*, the first emperor to rule Vietnam after its independence from China. The Hung Vuong Dynasty continued to rule in Vietnam for 2,622 years. Now, during each lunar new year's celebration, Vietnamese people all over the world hold a ceremony in memory of their first emperor.

The temple was colorful and bright. Proudly, Phuc Tran showed me the altar he had arranged with his own hands. The yellow chrysanthemums made me think of spring. There were bowls of oranges, tangerines, apples, and huge yellow grapefruits that were too large to hold in one hand. Here again, Phuc Tran wished me a Happy New Year.

Later that day, as I was standing on the fairgrounds with the smell of barbecued pork in the air, I listened to the sounds of people laughing, chatting, and humming to the Vietnamese music coming from the loudspeakers overhead. Surrounded by the sights and sounds of a country far away, I realized that although I have never been to Vietnam, it is a part of my heritage and a special part of my life.

Families visiting the TET Festival often wear traditional Vietnamese clothing. A woman and her daughter are dressed in their *ao dai*.

In celebrating this season of new beginnings, I share a tradition that dates back thousands of years.

My voice joins many others in saying
"Chuc Mung Nam Moi!"
(CHOOK MUNG NAM MOI)
Happy New Year!

INDEX

Numbers in *italics* refer to pages with photos.